WANT TO INVEST IN CRYPTOCURRENCIES?

Things to look out for before investing in any coin

ERNEST JONES

Copyright © Ernest Jones

All rights reserved. This book or any portion thereof may not be reproduced or used in any manner whatsoever without the express written permission of the publisher except for the use of brief quotations in a book review.

TABLE OF CONTENTS

INTRODUCTION

METHOD ONE

When Profits Are Too Good To Be True

METHOD TWO

Coins That Need Referrals to Gain Value

METHOD THREE

Coins That Have Unknown and Anonymous Ownership

METHOD FOUR

Coins That Entice You to Invest First Before You Can Know More

METHOD FIVE

Closed Source Codes

AKNOWLEDGEMENT

I wish to acknowledge my wife in her effort to keeping our home going. I can barely find the words to express all the love and support you've given me. You are my number one fan and for that I am eternally grateful. I wish to remain the best friend you've ever have. I Love You Darling!

INTRODUCTION

While it is difficult to predict the future of any cryptocurrency, what I know is that the popularity of cryptocurrencies is continually increasing. One of the reasons why cryptocurrencies are becoming more popular is because of the blockchain technology, which is the main technology behind all cryptocurrencies.

So many people have falling victim to the hype surrounding every cryptocurrency-bubble. There is always somebody captured by FOMO (fear of missing out), hence buying massively from almost every coin that comes out, just with the hope of making money quickly when they don't even understand what cryptocurrency is all about. That's a very bad idea. You don't have to continue this way. Get to know the red signs of fake coins before you invest your hard earned money.

* * * * * *

METHOD ONE

* * * * * *

When Profits Are Too Good To Be True

1,000% guaranteed return on your investment in just 3 months? Will double your investment by tomorrow?

If it sounds too good to be true, then it is not.

Genuine cryptocurrencies do not attempt to raise funds based on the potential returns on their investment. Instead, they take pleasure in their technology and target and **NOT** from the potential value of its currencies. This is, in general, the biggest revealing sign of a cryptocurrency Ponzi scheme. Normally, the higher the possible rate of return, the greater the risk. If the marketing campaign of a coin is just about promoting the value of the currency, stay away from it. Whether through cloud mining websites, investment programs or cryptocurrencies without true origin, no investment can generate high returns without risks or guaranteed returns.

If any crypto coin developer tries to sell itself promising benefits on its investments, run away.

* * * * * *

METHOD TWO

* * * * * *

Coins That Need Referrals to Gain Value

Have you ever heard about Ponzi scheme before? You may have heard about it or not. If a crypto coin needs more people to register and more investors to gain value, it is more than likely a pyramid or a Ponzi scheme.

If the major means to earn money from a coin is through referrals commissions, it is a Ponzi scheme.

Again, genuine Cryptocurrencies

don't grow by the number of people who have their currencies. They do it through accurate execution of their objectives, good teamwork and good technology. You don't have to participate or partake in their growth by getting more referral for the currency, that is not your work to do.

* * * * * *

METHOD THREE

* * * * * *

Coins That Have Unknown and Anonymous Ownership

Are the founders or the developers anonymous?

Any coin which has anonymous team or unknown owners is a sign of a red flag for you. Not having names means that there is no guarantee that the team will keep to its promises.

Also, any currency which has no detailed information about the team behind it is incomplete, to say the least. Even if there is a team behind it, conduct a thorough Google search of the people to verify their history. In recent months, there have been multiple ICOs directed or founded by individuals who have a history of fraud before, for example, defrauding investors with their money, money laundering and the theft of funds from cryptocurrency exchanges.

Invest only in currencies in which the team is reliable, highly qualified and respected by the community.

* * * * * *

METHOD FOUR

* * * * * *

Coins That Entice You to Invest First Before You Can Know More

Once more, any cryptocurrency that you need to invest first before getting more information show signs of a Ponzi scam. Genuine coins are always transparent in everything!

To bypass the radar of the authorities, so many scam crypto coin websites present themselves as legit businesses, such as rendering a wallet platform service, a market place or a cloud mining platform.

But, to get more information about the service, you must first invest or register as a member to get more information.

After you might have invested, the material and the focus of the website will seem to be different from their main focus, which is recruitment and "investment", exactly like a Ponzi scheme works!

* * * * * *

METHOD FIVE

* * * * * *

Closed Source Codes

Good and honest crypto companies have source code for their coins visible to the general public in some places like Github. Fake crypto companies, on the other hand keep their source code and backend information of their projects as hidden as possible.

For fraudulent coins, almost all of them have a closed source code, which means that the code behind the coins is not visible to the public. This is totally different from genuine coins like Ethereum, whereby 100% of their source code is available for the public to see through their Github profile. Likewise, fake coins can also have private blockchains to ensure that nobody, except them, has access to transactions in the blockchain. This goes against the initial vision of the blockchain to a public digital ledger. You can carry out a quick check to see if they are listed in CoinMarketCap (lthough many fake coins are listed there these days, so it's just a minor check) which requires coins to genuine, traded on a public exchange with an API available, and must have a public URL that shows the coin's total supply.

Thanks for reading!

www.ingramcontent.com/pod-product-compliance
Lightning Source LLC
Chambersburg PA
CBHW031601210526
45464CB00003B/1375